FRENCH MUSIC TODAY

Da Capo Press Music Reprint Series

FRENCH MUSIC TODAY

By Claude Rostand

*Translated from the French
by Henry Marx*

Da Capo Press · New York · 1973

Library of Congress Cataloging in Publication Data

Rostand, Claude.

   French music today.

   (Da Capo Press music reprint series)

   Translation of La musique française contemporaine.

   Reprint of the ed. published by Merlin Press, New York.

   1. Music—France. 2. Music—History and criticism—20th century. I. Title.

[ML270.5.R713   1973]   781.7'44   73-4333

ISBN 0-306-70578-8

This Da Capo Press edition of
French Music Today is an unabridged republication
of the 1955 edition published in New York.

Copyright © 1955 by Merlin Press, Inc.

Published by Da Capo Press, Inc.
A Subsidiary of Plenum Publishing Corporation
227 West 17th Street, New York, N.Y. 10011

FRENCH MUSIC TODAY

FRENCH

MUSIC

TODAY

Translated from the French by Henry Marx

CLAUDE ROSTAND

MERLIN PRESS-NEW YORK

Printed in Germany

CONTENTS

		Page
I.	Setting the Stage	11
II.	The Arceuil School	20
III.	La Jeune France ("Young France")	33
	a) Name, Action and Manifesto	33
	b) Messiaen	42
	c) Jolivet	67
	d) Lesur	73
	e) Baudrier	77
IV.	The Independents	81
	a) Background: Conservatoire .	83
	b) Others	95
V.	The Latest Trends	111
	a) The Independents	112
	b) The Progressivists . . .	119
	c) The Zodiaque	121
	d) The Dodekaphonists . . .	127
VI.	Conclusion	142

FRENCH MUSIC FOR...

FRENCH MUSIC TODAY

I

*T*HE MUSICAL STAGE OF France is filled with about a hundred players. There is a little bit of everything: big tenors, small parts, casts of the traditional repertory and actors with revolutionary techniques. However, this constitutes a rather good balance in the ensemble.

In a small book such as this we cannot possibly deal with every one of these hundred players. Nevertheless, it is possible to describe the principal personalities as well as the dominant trends in such a way as to give a fairly truthful survey of present day French music, one reflecting the various significant movements as they have evolved during our lifetime.

At the outset we shall try to link the present with the past and take a rapid inventory of the aesthetic facts and techniques which have influenced the work played before us.

The composers of our day are beneficiaries of the most fecund, the richest heritage ever. Between the birth of Cesar Franck (1822) and the death of Maurice Ravel (1937) the renaissance of the French school of music has led to what has been termed the Third Golden Age of our music. It encompassed three successive generations, that of Franck, Saint-Saëns, Gounod and Lalo; that of Fauré, Debussy, Dukas, d'Indy, Duparc and

Chabrier, and that of Ravel, Roussel and Schmitt. Alongside this ensemble, which constitutes the most important part of the heritage bequeathed our contemporaries (to which, as another essentially national influence, we have to add the *Group of Six),* mention must be made also of considerable foreign influences: Russian, Spanish, Middle European and Negro.

Considered from a strictly national viewpoint, work and attainments of the leaders of the Third Golden Age led to the rediscovery of French tradition. They had been nurtured, more or less abundantly, by Italian, German, Spanish and Slavic elements, which they quickly transcended, however.

The most important and decisive factors are:

Firstly, there is Fauré's exemplary harmony. "I have gone as far as possible within that which was allowed," he wrote.

Indeed, Fauré was not a revolutionary who violated traditional rules of chord succession. Together with his continued admiration for these traditional rules, however, he demonstrated how to speak an entirely new language.

Debussy was just the opposite. His was a radical revolution. He freed the elements of musical language from traditional fetters, as indicated in his unresolved dissonances, parallel octaves and fifths, etc. He reintroduced the use of certain scales other than the major and minor of the diatonic, such as whole-tone scales, Gregorian modes (unused since the end of the sixteenth century), and Chinese pentatonic scales. It was also to his merit that the Wagnerian question, a rather menacing one in the France of the beginning century, was solved — and that without repudiation of the attainments of the Wagnerian language. Finally, he left

14

us a new conception of music drama and a new manner of employment of the orchestral palette, one which, in the absolute terms of general music history, leads to the discoveries of Schoenberg and the Viennese School.

Thirdly — closer to us — there is Ravel with his extraordinary workmanship and his unheard-of harmonic subtleties. He, too, utilized other than the traditional scales, particularly certain Arab as well as Chinese and church modes. With incomparable skill he perfected Debussy's achievements in this domain, employing as he did these scales as a base for his melodies and thereby opening the door to an inexhaustible variety. Some of his works, the *Poèmes de Mallarmé,* for instance, suggest a real tonal disintegration, not as a result of true atonal consciousness, but rather as the outcome of an extremely complex manner of writing which embraced the ambiguity of tonality. Although the Ravel procedure is not atonal, one can say that the effect of atonal sound is present. Ravel suggests an unequaled case to newcomers, that of a genius reviving French classicism in its purest form as a result of an urge for discipline and sense for strict form; and this discipline and form never cease to hark back to dance as origin of music. He found particular resonance with the new composers for two reasons: his abhorrence of pathos and his lavishing care on rhythm. Finally, he bequeathed to posterity some orchestral techniques, better models even than Debussy's because they are more rational.

Besides these three there is Erik Satie's influence, more spiritual and aesthetic than purely musical. True, we owe certain innovations in the harmonic order to him, such as parallel ninths, etc., but it is primarily his anti-Debussyan mentality, his urge for the unembellished and the bare, his search for simplicity and for systematic nakedness, as it were, that have exercised an influence on the younger generations.

Two other composers, Paul Dukas and Vincent d'Indy, likewise have contributed to the bulk of our heritage today. They constitute an equilibrium, so to speak, primarily due to their romantic natures: the former emerges from diffuse and unadmitted postromanticism in which firm classical tendencies and impressionist aspirations either fight or complement one another; the latter is a romanticist of Germanic traditions but with pronounced French persuasion. Their effectiveness is not so much the result of their romantic mentality as it is their handling of the musical architecture. They exemplify general order, balance, good form and development, logic and breadth of composition.

In addition, two great currents from abroad have enriched the heritage of the young generation. Their origins are Stravinsky and Schoenberg. The Russian contributed, above all, antitonality which in turn opened the door to polytonality and atonality, and, in addition, to the emancipation of rhythm heretofore unknown in the history of music. The primitive power of *Sacre du Printemps* has played a decisive role in France. The Austrian's contribution is atonality and twelve-tone music organized on the basis of tone-rows or tone-series — both a radical revolution and the beginning of a natural evolution. We will later appraise the extent to which French musicians have utilized the suggestions of Schoenberg.

Finally there is the *Group of Six*. They

have not been included in this survey of present day French music so as to keep our survey brief and because the exploits of the *Six* are well known. Much as the *Group of Six* is the result of its predecessors, it is also a reaction against them. These composers were catalyzers. It is due to them that certain nonconformist aesthetic attitudes and certain revolutionary technical procedures have exerted an influence on the young composers, even though the latter would not always acknowledge such patronage. Irrespective of the value — more or less great — of the output of each individual of the *Six*, collectively their work was necessary. It has had a wholesome effect on the French school because of its novel atmosphere and a new humanism. These came at a time when the French school showed tendencies of becoming ossified in rigidly academic formulae.

II

*I*T CANNOT BE SAID THAT what we nowadays term the *Arceuil School* had real life, dogmatically or doctrinally. It is rather but a "moment" in the history of contemporary French music that we characterize by this term. As in the case of the *Six* it is a handy label, one which apparently has survived despite elements of inconsistency. With such a term obviously we cannot hope to describe the art of the composers in question, nor can we characterize the role played by each one of them, for it is certain that neither temporary enthusiasm nor transitory confirmation of a fairly vague kinship of taste suffice to constitute a "school." It seems that the term *Arceuil School* was intended by its members as homage to Erik Satie rather than the expression of their intention to form an effective group of disciples.

Toward the end of his life Erik Satie stayed in Arceuil, a small locality within Greater Paris. Three of the *Six* who had been under his influence, Milhaud, Auric and Poulenc, had reached a point where they considered their artistic ideas and their successes their own. Meanwhile a new group of young people formed around him, among them Henri Sauguet, Maxime Jacob, Henri Cliquet-Pleyel and Roger Désormière. "You must march alone," he told them. "Don't do as I did. Listen to nobody!" They marched alone, they did not copy him, and they were right.

The only common idea discernible in these four young artists during that time was their admiration for the old master of Arceuil and a tendency toward systematic simplicity in music — not altogether opposed to the will which had animated the *Six*, but which apparently was strengthened under Satie's influence as a reaction against what until then may have appeared excessive.

Of these four musicians, two have produced but little, Henri Cliquet-Pleyel and Roger Désormière. The latter has written movie music but has left a mark particularly as a conductor by dedicating himself heart and soul to the defense of contemporary music. He has conducted a great number of world premières and deserves the gratitude of musicians of all countries. A serious ailment now keeps him from the conductor's platform, and doubtlessly will for a long time to come; this is a great misfortune for modern music.

Quite a different individual is Maxime Jacob who, of Jewish descent, embraced Catholicism, became a Bendictine monk and the organist of his monastery. He has continued to compose under the name of Dom Clément. Darius Milhaud, a friend of his, wrote that Maxime Jacob as a young man contributed particular freshness and lightness to the *Arceuil School.* The first period of his creative work, plain in inspiration and construction, is completely in harmony with the aesthetic principles of simplicity as pursued by the group. His *Overture,* his stage music for *Voulez-vous jouer avec moi?,* his *Sérénade* for string quartet and wind instruments, his songs based on poems by Musset, Verlaine, Derême, Cocteau, René

Chalupt, etc. — they all show charm, clarity, simplicity, and sound like a rather awkward tribute to the art of a Gounod whom the group liked to claim as its ancestor, more than to that of one of the great revolutionaries of the twentieth century.

Since joining the religious order Jacob has dedicated himself to the composition of sacred music, trying to eschew the vulgarity all too frequently found in that field. He endeavors to adhere, as closely as possible, to Gregorian melody and the Palestrina type of polyphony, and to find an expression worthy of the place of worship. He writes in such a way that these works can be mastered by small church choirs *(Douze Cantiques de Fête)*. In this way he has remained true in his life and his art to the ideals of humility and utter simplicity which brought the young men of the *Arceuil School* together.

Henri Sauguet is the most important of these four. At the outset his efforts were encouraged by Darius Milhaud, who introduced him to Satie. He later became a pupil of Canteloube and Koechlin. If his early works are not always devoid of a certain awkwardness, they nevertheless betray the expressive poetic power which never diminishes in the works of his maturity. He was quickly accepted by the musical world. He composed works for the theatre (ballets and comic operas) for the performances or Beriza, Diaghileff, Count de Beaumont, Ida Rubinstein and Serge Lifar (*Le Plumet du Colonel, La Chatte, David la Nuit, La Contrebasse,* etc.).

Simultaneously with these first works for the theatre Sauguet tried his hand at chamber music (the *Françaises,* the Piano Sonata, *Pièces Poétiques* for piano, the Sonatina for flute and piano, the *Divertis-*

sement de Chambre for five instruments) and, most of all, at many songs to poems by Louise Labé, Schiller, Swinburne, Gautier, Jean Paul and Heine.

In this formative period Sauguet's language already is highly personal, particularly so with respect to melodic invention. However, strangely enough, the recognition of influence or influences to which he might have been exposed in this early production is most difficult; in his later compositions they are easier to determine.

A period of transition followed. While Sauguet's musical language loses nothing of its originality and its highly personal flavor, it becomes stronger and subtler at the same time and frees itself of the clumsiness which — though on occasion not without a certain wayward charm — burdens his early works. This period falls in the thirties. There is the Concerto for piano and orchestra, the brilliant and clear instrumental style of which offers formidable technical difficulties for the soloist; *La Voyante,* a cantata for voice and small orchestra, one of Sauguet's most original and frequently acclaimed scores; *Les Ombres du Jardin,* for four voices, small choir and chamber orchestra, and particularly *La Chartreuse de Parme,* an opera in four acts and eleven scenes (Paris Opera, 1939), on a libretto by Armand Lunel. Sauguet, always attracted by the theatre, makes his most important contribution to the lyric theatre with this work — his most important, but not necessarily of uniform quality. Obviously, it was quite a risk for a librettist to draw, from Stendhal's grandiose masterwork, a libretto which had to be an entity from the psychological point of view and could at the same time be molded into an evening of opera. Lunel made the best of it, even though he was compelled to extreme simplification, and that compulsion probably has deprived certain episodes of their full breadth and dramatic intensity. The poetic range so characteristic of the composer predominates, and we find pages which communicate intense emotion without recourse to superficial effects or theatrical formulae (such as the prison scenes, the duo of Sanseverina and de Mosca on the shores of Lake Como, the sermon in the church, the latter being one of the most difficult imaginable by its very nature, yet one in which Sauguet succeeds with remarkable tact and ingenuity). Despite its expressive qualities, which are so prominent, the work failed to meet with its deserved success, and colleagues and critics hastened to expose certain awkward passages of the score which undeniably exist. They maligned the orchestration and criticized the stylistic unevenness. The audience at the *Opéra,* fond of grand effects, was misled by the discretion, sobriety, simplicity and the lack of routine in a work which perhaps had not quite broken with the traditional clichés of romantic opera, but which had both the courage and the virtue of voluntarily denying itself cheap recourse to the obvious.

Since the forties, Sauguet has written a number of works in all fields in which he has shown himself the possessor of a style, a musical language and an orchestral palette more and more assertive and homogeneous. One observes the influence of the Stravinsky of the *Jeux de Cartes* in this period, an influence which remains very light and, while real, in no way encroaches upon the originality of Sauguet's musical discourse. This phase includes *La Gageure Imprévue,* a little comic opera after Sedaine; *Les Forains,* a ballet which, with the admirable scenery by Christian Bérard, has several times toured the world triumphantly, and in which the composer strikingly evokes the melancholy milieu of the poor tent circus — Sauguet at his best; *La Rencontre d' Oedipe et du Sphinx,* a ballet in which the Stravinsky influence is particularly discernible; the *Symphonie Expiatoire,* dedicated to the innocent victims of the war, a deeply touching homage, possessing much grandeur without ever being rhetorical, and *Les Saisons,* an allegoric symphony, first presented as a radio oratorio, then as a ballet — a score replete with the poetry of nature. Finally, there is a whole series of songs on poems by Rilke, Heine, Hoelderlin, Baudelaire, Mallarmé and Laforgue.

Sauguet's predilection for the romanticists is reflected in these names. His temperament seems to carry him toward a certain sentimental expressionism, toward the secrets of the heart. "It's from within," he said, "that music must seek to understand and to move us as modern people." Yet he never indulges in the excesses of the great romanticists. He is a classic at heart. He possesses the moderation, sobriety, harmony and clarity which are among the traditionally consistent qualities of French genius. His aesthetic attitude brings to mind predecessors of German romanticism like Weber, to whom music first of all was poetry.

The originality of Sauguet's melodic ingenuity has often been commented upon, but his rhythms are no less personal in that he makes no point of subtle or complex combinations — therefore his undisputed success in the field of ballet. With respect to harmony, there is no particular innovation: although never impersonal it is of a somewhat exaggerated simplicity in his first works, probably as a result of Satie's influence. It has constantly become richer, more colorful, stronger and more refined without, however, losing any of its clarity and transparency. Always remaining solidly attached to the principle of tonality, it is *sans* studied aggressiveness. However, it makes full use of a harmonic vocabulary which bears the stamp of its time.

III

*T*HE TERM LA JEUNE FRANCE, just as the "groups" or "schools" heretofore discussed, is not supposed to indicate a particular systematic technique which its members would have in common. On the contrary, the group is most heterogeneous. Its unity derives only from general aspirations and tendencies which are aesthetic and essentially extramusical, thus in no way affecting purely technical solutions. Most of all, it is a movement founded in 1936 in reaction against the abstract tendencies of middle European composers as represented in the *Triton,* Paris's society of contemporary music.

The prime mover in the group is Yves Baudrier. In 1935 when listening to Olivier Messiaen's *Offrandes Oubliées* in a concert at the *Conservatoire,* he "suddenly became aware of the spiritual movement which had taken hold of many young artists in France." Baudrier contacted Messiaen and they agreed on the common pursuit of their ideals. Messiaen thereupon proposed the formation of a group together with two young composer friends who were as yet unbeknown to one another: André Jolivet and Daniel Lesur. Both had already given proof of their dynamic vitality with regard to the problems of contemporary music in concerts of the *Société Nationale,* the *Société Internationale de Musique Con-*

temporaine, as well as of the *Spirale* and the *Orchestre Symphonique de Paris.*

In Baudrier's basement apartment, where disorder supreme reigned over books, scores and records, these four musicians of most differing backgrounds met to collate their ideas and plans. Messiaen and Lesur had been graduated from the Paris Conservatory, Jolivet had chosen his teachers for their individual theories, and Baudrier was self-taught.

The following manifesto as printed in the program of the first concert of this group on June 3, 1936 at the *Salle Gaveau* was born from their deliberations:

"As living conditions become more and more hard, mechanical and impersonal, music must bring its spiritual fortitude and its generous reactions to those who love it. *La Jeune France,* reviving a term created by Berlioz a long time ago,

35

pursues the road upon which the master once took his obdurate course. We are a group of four friends, all young French composers: Olivier Messiaen, Daniel Lesur, André Jolivet and Yves Baudrier. *La Jeune France* has for its goal the dissemination of young free works equally removed from revolutionary and academic formulae.

"The tendencies of this group will be diverse, but we do agree that our satisfaction can be only in sincerity, generosity and critical conscience. Our aim is to create and to foster a *living* music.

"At each concert *La Jeune France,* acting as an unbiased jury, will arrange that, within its modest means, one or several works characteristic of some interesting trend within the bounds of its aspirations will be performed.

"*La Jeune France* also hopes to encourage the young French school which has been allowed to languish through the indifference or the penury of official powers. It will allow the music of the great composers of the past to continue in this century for they have made French music one of the purest jewels of civilization."

One may well add to the words sincerity, generosity and conscience, which in some way became the motto of this group, the words literature, philosophy and humanism. Literature and philosophy are the preoccupation in the work of at least three of these four musketeers, Daniel Lesur being the only one to escape this extramusical involvement. Let us state right here that these literary or philosophical preoccupations are often so awkwardly expressed that, no matter how touching, they frequently remain infantile if not primitive. In this sense the evocation of Berlioz and the use of the romantic label *La Jeune France* are fully justified.

The idea of humanism as emanating from this movement is its most interesting feature. Apart from what we find in the work of each one of these four composers, this feature has been expressly stated by Yves Baudrier who, all in all, has been the thinker, editor and mouthpiece of the group. He defines the common program as a return to lyricism and humanism. Similarly, André Jolivet wrote, "I am more and more convinced that the mission of musical art is humane and religious (in the sense of *re-ligare*)."

Here we find one of those "returns," one of the reactions which periodically appear in the history of music when, following former reactions or "returns to . . . ", contemporaries consider it their duty to react against excessive or extremist mentalities or doctrines which have established themselves and have become habits. This attempt of this group at "the reincarnation of music in man" was undoubtedly natural and desirable between the two wars, and to form a solid group for that purpose was useful. However, this group unquestionably was a mixture of systematic progressivism (Messiaen, Jolivet), of humanist tradition (Lesur), and of pure instinct (Baudrier).

La Jeune France remained confined to its four members whose instincts, tastes, goals and musical personalities admitted neither limitation nor regimentation. It is easily conceivable, though, that among the composers to be discussed in the following chapters there are some who could have broadened the ranks of this vanguard. At one time the name of Jehan Alain was mentioned as a likely affiliate of the cause. Generally speaking, the group was far from enshrining itself in an ivory tower; on the contrary, at each of its concerts it welcomed a musician who did not "belong," particularly Germaine Tailleferre, Claude Arrieu, Marcel Delannoy, Georges Dandelot, Georges Migot, Tony Aubin, Henri Martelli, Jean Françaix, J. J. Gruenenwald, etc.

The fact that they had become a group in all likelihood had no real influence on the purely musical aspect of their work, but it did enable the four composers to become better known by joining forces. Their efficient publicity (a word not used derogatorily) was evident from their very first concert: everybody was afraid that nobody would come; as a result all musical Paris, always a bit sadistic, came in order to have it confirmed that nobody had come.

La Jeune France consequently made its debut before one of the largest and most distinguished audiences imaginable. The battle was won even before the first fight. The next morning the critics — comprised of either journalists or fellow composers — were unanimous in celebrating "the four little brothers in spirit," in declaring that they were beloved "because they say strongly and stubbornly what they have to say" and that they "are the leaders of that current of lofty thought which enjoyably regenerates young French music."

These four musicians typify, so to speak, the principal aspects and solutions of a problem which inevitably is posed by the entire evolution of music: on the one hand, there are those who believe it essential first to attempt a reorganization of the expressive means (Messiaen and Jolivet); on the other, there are those who think that the search for a musical vocabulary should not be the primary concern, and that that search in fact is responsible for the gap which for years has existed between the public and the composer (Lesur and Baudrier).

———

OLIVIER MESSIAEN, born December 10, 1908 at Avignon, was a remarkably precocious boy. He entered the Paris Conservatory at the age of eleven, his musical bent having manifested itself four years previously in the writing of small pieces. He was graduated with highest honors after having completed the courses of Jean and Noël Gallon in harmony, counterpoint and fugue, Marcel Dupré in organ and Paul Dukas in composition. Since 1931 he has been organist at the Trinity Church in Paris and professor at the *Ecole Normale de Musique,* the *Schola Cantorum* and at his alma mater, the *Conservatoire* (harmony, and later analysis, aesthetics and rhythm).

In the two years following World War II a public controversy raged over what became known as "the case Messiaen." It was sustained with violence in praise as well as in criticism. Everyone indulged in it to his heart's content: this may be explained as an immediate result of the return of freedom of expression. Today, looking back over those years, it is easy to determine the harvest of that freedom: if one or the other party in that controversy indulged in excesses or foolishness, the resulting mound of writings gives us at least a chance to appraise the matter from every possible viewpoint. Music critics kindled all sorts of conflagrations. The composers, of whom it was least expected, entered the fray, thereby surprising everybody since they had not been in the habit of publicizing good or bad opinions on colleagues. The snobbishness of the "happy few" also played a role, and even part of the public at large, half amused and half interested, went to the hustings to air its opinion in a blundering, incoherent but sincere way, as is to be expected under such circumstances. "The case Messiaen" had assumed the proportions of full warfare.

Amusingly enough, there never was a "case Messiaen." What was taken for it were some random manifestations. These corresponded in degree with the inspiration of fanatics who were either in full agreement with one or the other side. As it is, the only "case Messiaen" has been the one of a richly endowed artist who, like all artists of great temperament, tries to express what this temperament dictates to him, and who at the same time also searches for the means of expression believed to be novel. Without being critical, it seems that Messiaen is more of an explorer and juggler than an inventor in the plain sense of the word. He is an artist who, by making use of the elements of an existing musical language — to be sure combining them in a novel way and bringing them to perfection — has tried to express only one feeling. This feeling constitutes the novelty of Messiaen's contribution rather than do the means of expression he employs. The feeling creates the impression of novelty even more so since it derives from a temperament of exceptional ardor, although one can very well envision the quality of this ardor.

It is this point which leads us to an investigation of some of the characteristic aspects of his aesthetics on the one hand and his musical language on the other.

At the time of "the case Messiaen" a reporter, interviewing him on his preferences and disappointments, asked him, "Does faith in your art sustain you?"

"The faith, and only the faith," the composer answered. "I am, above all, a Catholic composer. All my works, whether religious or not, are documents of faith glorifying the mystery of Christ. Through my poor stammerings about Divine Love I have tried to find a music signifying a new epoch, a loving and chanting music."

Elsewhere he says:

"As a child I was irresistibly attracted to the Catholic faith, music, the theatre and its scenery. Only the first two passions have endured. I have tried to be a Christian musician singing of his faith — without ever accomplishing it, undoubtedly because I have not been worthy of it, and that I say without false humility! In my work pure, secular and sacred music alternate. The sacred music is not as mystic as the majority of my listeners believe. I really don't know whether I have an 'aesthetic code,' but I may say that my preference is for a florid, refined, even voluptuous music, but never sensuous, to be sure. Mine is a music that soothes and sings, does justice to melody and to the melodic phrase, a music of new blood, of definite gesture, like unknown scents, like restless birds, a music like stained glass windows, a turning wheel of complementary colors. My wish is to express in music the end of time, ubiquity, glorious hosts, divine and metaphysical mysteries, a rainbow within the sacred realm, so to speak.

47

"When I said all this in the *Salle Gaveau* in commenting on my *Vingt Regards sur l'Enfant Jésus,* the critics made fun of me. Were they perhaps right? In religious matters a good deed is more important than a symphony, a clean life better than a work of art."

In another passage Messiaen states:

"I want to write music which is an act of faith, music that touches all subjects, without ever ceasing to touch God... In order to express with constant force our darkness in combat with the Holy Spirit, in order to open the doors of our prison of human flesh and reveal the heights, in order to give our century the blessed water which it needs, one must be a great artist and at the same time a great craftsman and a great Christian."

"Darkness," "prison of human flesh": these with a thousand others are words indicating Olivier Messiaen's essentially religious engrossment, perhaps with all the complications they imply. His ideal is the great artist, the great craftsman, the great Christian of whom he speaks: this makes the source of his inspiration abundantly clear.

Messiaen has written a great deal about his work and himself. These writings, while resulting in some confusion, also offer some supplementary and very useful and precise facts. He never said that he believed to be this ideal himself or that he could ever become one. Rather, his religious sense renders such contention impossible. In the face of attacks or misinterpretations he emphasizes that his music should be considered sacred rather than mystic, and indeed that is justified also in view of the system and organization of his musical discourse. Messiaen has explained his belief in the meaning of inspiration and in what way it expresses itself in his own work. This explanation, not without beauty, merits quotation here for it is important for the comprehension of the artist and his work.

"Inspiration is like death: it hovers everywhere around us, in the mountains, in a church window, in a book on medicine, astronomy or microphysics. Some seek it by praying to God, others by embracing a woman. The musician finds music in all things. For a lover all things have that color which the lover sees in them. What hidden vibrations, mysterious symphonies does one find in a cloud, a star or a child's eye! I believe in musical inspiration. Not that kind which brusquely invades with Pythian ecstasy, rather one which takes shape despite us through slow, imperceptible effort, and that inspiration haunts and possesses us. It is like a fixed idea, just as is love. *Inspiration is like love.* Often it makes fun of us. One sets out with the intention of writing music for the theatre, he ends with twenty piano pieces; one would like to write songs, but the result is a symphonic poem or an act of an opera. But why try to draw aside the veil before inspiration's secrets, before its puzzling smiles? All I can confirm is that I can write nothing which I have not lived."

This is not the place to find out to what extent Messiaen's message is truly Christian. The church has pronounced no verdict on this subject. However, one can quote the testimony of several authorities in the field of religious art, such as Henri Davenson, Dom Clément Jacob and Reverend Father Florant who offer widely differing reactions of interest to those concerned about the "faint sulphuric odor" of this music and who want to stay aloof from it. To Davenson, Messiaen "is suspect of swindling with mysticism," and he observes that "there is no true music whatever without asceticism, while the first ascetic practice is silence." He asks whether the opulence of such art does not produce "too earthy a music considering the mystical values with which Messiaen pretends to surfeit it."

Jacob is explicit in saying that "Messiaen's work is boldly, clearly and openly Catholic and mystical," but he takes no notice of the affinity which is possible between an art so "voluptuously refined" and theology. As far as Florant is concerned, he cares little that Messiaen's art is more or less a manifestation of hedonism, and he has no hesitation in stating that the composer has "written his name into the record of full-blooded Christian humanity."

The same Florant declares: "Messiaen is a great musician who can be explained beyond what he writes in notes." Without insistence on this explanation, he accounts for the literary and poetic aspects of the composer. Messiaen has always surrounded his works with comments to explain what he wanted to say and how he has said it. Subjected to ambient and uninhibited verbosity by his mother, the poetess Cécile Sauvage, authoress of *L'Ame en Bourgeon,* he uses a poetic and rather baroque language for the explanation of his musical intentions:

"My secret desire has pushed me toward these fire-swords, these flashing stars, these streams of blue and orange

lava, these turquoise planets, these vio-
lets, these garnets of hairy arborescence,
these changes in sounds and colors in a
mass of rainbows, etc. . . . " Examples of
this sort need not be added. He even goes
as far as to invent language in which "each
syllable has been chosen for its tenderness
or its timbre or with respect to its value
as musical rhythm." *(Harawi)* It should
also be noted — and this is by no means
unimportant for the formation of his mind
as well as his feelings — that when quite
young he lived with Shakespeare's char-
acters as though they were real persons.
His father was a remarkable Shakespeare
translator.

There is first the man Messiaen, and
then the believer and the poet. Only then
there is the musician of inordinate culture. In his own admission, his music is
principally influenced by the following:
Debussy, Dukas, Berg, Jolivet, Stra-

vinsky, Rimsky-Korsakoff and Moussorgsky. Debussy's influence, very strong in Messiaen's early work, lingers on, if only in the inclination to capture voluptuous and iridescent clusters. Paul Dukas is a more spiritual than real influence, and *Ariane et Barbe-Bleue* seems to have played a certain role because of its symbolism, through its gem scenes, etc. Then follows Alban Berg. In André Jolivet we have probably the only case of reciprocal influence between the members of *La Jeune France.* It is rather strange that such an influence should be important with those of the four who are most original, independent and personal; perhaps it can generally be considered a sign of strength for anyone to accept influence without fear of confinement. Whatever the reason, the influence is there, and Messiaen's commentary on André Jolivet's *Mana,* a piece of unabashed admiration, is quite indicative of it. There remain Stravinsky, Rimsky-Korsakoff and Moussorgsky. As regards theory, Messiaen retained much of the instruction also of Jean and Noël Gallon and their theory of *Harmonie Véritable*, latent in his melody, of Marcel Dupré's teaching of counterpoint and Maurice Emmanuel's of the evolution of musical language.

His broad education made him conscious, even more acutely, of the necessity for the search for a new musical vocabulary. To the material commonly employed by Western composers, the systems of the chromatic and the diatonic scales with major and minor and the old Gregorian modes he added Indian music, the song of the birds and quarter tones.

Thus he coined a large musical alphabet for his own use. With it he established a tonal system upon which he elaborates in a brochure entitled *La Technique de mon Langage Musical*. He summarizes it as follows:

"The technique of my musical language rests mainly on two procedures: non-reversible rhythms and keys with limited transpositions. These keys effect vertically (transposition) what the rhythms effect horizontally (retrogression). Indeed, the keys cannot be transposed above a certain number of transpositions, or else they will turn into the same notes (enharmonically speaking); likewise, the rhythms cannot be read in reverse without representing the succession of values in the original direction. Other peculiarities of my technique are: augmented or diminished note values, notes added to basic chords, augmented or diminished rhythms, pedal points, passing notes, embellishments and upbeats. Since style is the blood and the very life of its author there are changes, and each change brings about new means of expression. Thus I have used, in the works following my treatise, rhythmic canons *(Vision de l'Amen),* augmented canons, a subtle type of polymodality *(Trois Petites Liturgies),* solid or broken chords, developments by means of changing the register, asymmetric augmentations, lengthened or shortened note values in succession *(Vingt Regards).* Furthermore, my last work contains a large number of sonorities, sound effects including harmonies which are new, as entities as well as in their juxtaposition. As a result, in some ten years I should be able to write a second treatise which would add abundantly to the first."

The organization of this technical system was built up, as in the case of Schoenberg, only by experience and experimentation. Both were animated by the composer's instinct which he himself defines as follows:

> "I search for a sparkling music which would give voluptuously refined pleasure to the ear ... [In other words, in this respect, there is still kinship to Debussyan feeling.] In a concert the listener will submit to the music, first will merely be charmed in order gradually to be led toward that kind of theological rainbow which the musical language tries to be and from which we seek to derive edification ... "

Messiaen tries to find "a new language which shall remain the factual and original expression of a period and a personality." Even though his immediate

59

predecessors, Debussy in particular, had come very close to that concept, it was by all means necessary to come still closer, and that explains the accumulation of matériel and other complexity toward which Messiaen was driven. He has been accused of being a slave to theory and justifies himself as follows:

"Never have I intentionally subjected myself to a compositional system. I use keys and rhythms automatically and arbitrarily and cannot understand how it could be different. Why forbid this or that? Sometimes I prefer to use major scales pure or mixed or in contrast with my own scales. At other times I like to imitate the singing of birds or Indian ragas. Then again I like to use twelve-tone technique all of a sudden because all at once I need it. I have done enough work in harmony at the *Conservatoire,* as student and later as teacher, to be permitted the freedom of writing as my imagination dictates and according to the exigencies of the subject matter, the musical subject, the instrumentation and the feeling of the moment."

Such an approach results in an extremely rich language, often too rich, and Messiaen's harmonic and rhythmic plenitude often produces something not clearly distinguishable, and consequently monotonous, the effects neutralizing each other. Melodically, however, it seems that the many resources which Messiaen has at his disposal by means of various scales have not been as fully exploited as could have been expected. In this respect the composer's predilection for the two melodic intervals of the augmented fourth and major sixth is to be noted.

Form and construction apparently have

not been of particular concern to Messiaen. Paul Dukas had already remarked that they were his student's weak points. In *La Technique de mon Lang age Musical* Messiaen devotes six chapters to rhythm, four to melody and three to harmony, but only one deals with musical form. We find little solicitude for the exigencies of form not only in these brief comments, but even more so in the compositions themselves, and yet the problem of musical form heavily weighs on all Western music throughout the ages, not excluding twelve-tone music in its most recent manifestations.

In contrast, Messiaen has given proof of an extraordinary refinement in orchestration which is comparable to his harmonic and rhythmic facilities. His works, moreover, in this respect testify to an ever-growing complexity discernible in the considerable development from the

Petites Liturgies to the *Turangalîla* symphony. Messiaen soon augmented the traditional orchestral palette with *Ondes Martenot* and some instruments borrowed from the Far East. Here, for example, are his comments concerning the orchestration in the last named work:

"Besides the traditional woodwinds and the string quintet the scoring of the *Turangalîla* symphony is highly varied. In the brass section the horns, trombones and tuba are joined by an important set of trumpets (a small D trumpet, three C trumpets and a B-flat cornet). The three keyboard instruments (glockenspiel, celesta and vibraphone) have been assigned a special role similar to the Indian *gamelan* as used in Indonesia (Java and Bali). The extensive percussion provides true rhythmic counterpoint. It consists of triangle, temple-block, wood-block, little Turkish cymbals, Chinese cymbals, gong, Basque tambourine, maracas, tambourine Provençal, tenor drum, bass drum, and eight bells. Furthermore, *Ondes Martenot* dominates the orchestra with its expressive timbre. Finally a piano solo part of greatest difficulty, used to brighten up the orchestra with its brilliant dashes, its clustered harmonies, its singing of birds, makes the *Turangalîla* symphony almost a concerto for piano and orchestra."

In his last works Messiaen branches out in an unexpected direction, thereby considerably enlarging his creative horizon. We have in mind, on the one hand, *Livre d'Orgue* and, on the other, two symphonic works, a concerto for piano and orchestra with the title *Le Réveil des*

Oiseaux ("The Awakening of the Birds") and a piece for orchestra with piano obbligato, named *Oiseaux Exotiques* ("Exotic Birds"). The composer in these three works attains a commendable synthesis which gives his art an entirely new physiognomy. This synthesis is a result, in part, of his own original findings, specifically his research on the keys and rhythms found in birdcalls, on the keys and rhythms of India, and on the modifications of certain principles of twelve-tone music. Messiaen does not become an exponent of twelve-tone music, but by uniting certain implications and potentialities of the Schoenberg method with his own specific technique, which had tended to limit him, he opens for himself numerous perspectives in expression.

In another of his recent works, *Quatre Etudes de Rythme* for piano solo, he combines scales of thirty-six tones with temporal and rhythmic values of twenty-four varieties in one and the same piece, and adds to them differentiations in dynamics and in attack. This work of such a novel and complex technique and structure has had a profound influence on many young European twelve-tone adherents.

Messiaen the teacher, with all his powerful personality, has scarcely had the supposedly destructive influence attributed to him. Basically his is a somewhat introverted and subdued temperament. According to his pupils, he failed to make an impression commensurate with the individuality of his works. On the other hand, they have nothing but praise for the keenness and objectivity with which he speaks of the great classics and with the approach he brings to the analysis of their works.

Even though it is difficult and dangerous to prophesy in such matters, it does not seem probable that Messiaen will exert a determining influence as a musician. If one may venture an opinion, one can define his role as that of a seeker whose achievements, at least in part, the future will utilize. He is a seeker much more than the head of a musical movement or a master of musical thought. This at least is the opinion of some of his own pupils who have the most profound and genuine veneration for him.

Indeed, does not the contribution of musical building material constitute a glorious role in the history of music?

———

ANDRE JOLIVET, born in Paris August 8, 1905, studied harmony, counterpoint and fugue with Paul le Flem, and

CLAUDE ROSTAND

composition, orchestration and acoustics
with Edgar Varèse. He is now conductor
at the *Comédie Française.*

As early as 1937, Messiaen, in a
justifiably enthusiastic article, defined
Jolivet's position in the music of our time
thusly:

"Is music ahead of the other arts?
One is forced to answer, no. No, it is
not ahead, it is pitifully, woefully,
stupidly lagging. This is normal and
it has always been that way but
never before has its delay been as
obvious. That's why we must ener-
getically support those — and it is a
very small number, three or four in
the whole world — who try to gain
a foothold. I have just read a work, a
simple suite for piano, which through
the novelty of its writing and the
uniqueness of its aesthetics seems
to be in accord with these goals. I am

speaking of André Jolivet's *Mana.*"
Jolivet's attitude is indeed characterized by a constant desire to advance
expressive means — and in that he is
basically comparable to Messiaen. However, while the latter operates, as it were,
in a closed circuit, Jolivet's is open. A
quick look at his work makes us distinguish — and here we generalize — two
main periods: one with incantation, the
other with humanity dominating, and
both corresponding to his own comment:
"I have become ever more convinced that
the mission of musical art is humane and
religious."

He contends that ever since 1935 he
has been trying to reinstate to music its
original, ancient meaning. In olden times
music was magical expression, incantation born from the expression of religious
fervor of peoples. At that moment he
composed *Mana,* a suite of six pieces for

the piano (Mana, Jolivet states, is the power perpetuating our well-known fetishes); *Cinq Incantations* for flute; *Cinq Danses Rituelles* and *Cosmogonie* for orchestra; *Danse Incantatoire* for orchestra with two *Ondes Martenot* and large percussion. In his own words, he seeks in these compositions a music which is "a manifestation in sound evolved from the direct relationship to the system of the universe." In his own admission he thereby wanted to free his technique from a tonal system. He did not want to adopt the theory of the chromatic scale, which ignores the natural phenomena of sound, but rather use just some of the twelve half-steps, particularly the most removed, with all their overtones. This led to new procedures of modulation, to the abandonment of the customary principles of four-part writing, to the establishment of a dynamic concept of sonority which would complete the elements of rhythm (this, according to him, is not just mere repetition of metric formulae or the ups and downs of lyricism, but is determined equally by phrases and by the intensity of the moving sound). Jolivet adds that all this research, if it is to produce valid results, must never cease to rely upon human feeling. Neither must it degenerate into virtuosity, into unmotivated play or into a complexity which would remove music from its main principle, which is the singing of human beings.

This concern apparently characterizes the second part of Jolivet's output. He does not abandon the symbolic and esoteric elements which, according to him, are essential in any work of art, but he no longer seeks to create works of cosmic significance. Instead, he returns to the humane, and by using a modal language composes scores of utmost spontaneity. This is evident, for example, in *Trois Chants des Hommes* for baritone and orchestra, and *Trois Complaintes du Soldat* for the same scoring.

His predilection for research in sonorities again is stressed in his latest works: Concerto for *Ondes Martenot* and orchestra, Concerto for trumpet and orchestra, Concerto for piano and orchestra. Particularly in the latter score, where Jolivet uses elements borrowed from tropical music (Africa, Far East and Polynesian Islands), he has tried to effect a compromise between the traditional language of tropical countries and present day tendencies of our Western. In the process he has systematically emphasized the phenomenon of orientalizing Western music, a movement begun, more or less instinctively, by Debussy. Debussy thereby considerably widened the range of our music and Bartok built on that basis intentionally and emphasized it further. Trying to integrate these two traditions, the European and the primitive-tropical, and therefrom to derive a homogeneous aesthetics, Jolivet attempted to create a universal language which would move equally Europeans, the black and the yellow races. He has endeavored to go even farther than Bartok in this direction. This is clear from his last works whose language, while actually universal, stems from popular traditions and is addressed only to a cultural elite in the West.

Viewed as a whole, his language, which for a time had been marked by the influence of Edgar Varèse and particularly of Alban Berg, acquired complete personality and originality. It is essentially based on the use of certain modes.

———

DANIEL LESUR was born in Paris

November 19, 1908. After studies at the Paris *Conservatoire* with Caussade (harmony, counterpoint and fugue), Tournemire (composition and organ) and Ferté (piano), he became assistant organist at St. Clothilde and professor of counterpoint at the *Schola Cantorum*. He was the teacher of almost all the musicians of the Zodiaque group and is presently a musical adviser to the *Radiodiffusion Française (Nouvelles Musicales)*.

To an inquiry made after World War II as to his aesthetic and technical principles, Lesur answered simply, but with singular precision in a manner which sheds light on his artistic personality, "Music is above all." His principles of style? "It all depends: music in verse or music in prose." What systematic principles of writing? "Why should anyone be so mean to himself?" Inspiration? "The heart has its own reasons which reason ignores." Otherwise, he declares: "One thing alone counts — that music contains much music. And in order to accomplish that, human must not be inhuman." Therefore he, too, comes close to the basic tendencies of *La Jeune France* and more particularly to those tendencies which embrace the romantic spirit.

His musical development seems shaped by an urge for freedom and development of his own temperament. During his first period he emerges as a classic haunted by concern for counterpoint. He was then about twenty-five, and wrote the *Suite Française* for orchestra and the *Passacaille* for piano and orchestra, works with clarity as uppermost concern and reflecting his desire to escape academic formulae. Then followed a period characterized by the sensualism inherent in the works written in his thirties, particularly the song cycles on poems by Claude Roy and Cécile Sauvage, and the *Chansons Cambodgiennes*. The third period seems to lead him toward a certain either dramatic or psychological form of romanticism. For the former one can quote *Andrea del Sarto*, vigorously orchestrated and of an incontestible dramatic dynamism; for the latter, the *Ballade* for piano which betrays a delicate, frank and sometimes quite ardent emotion without ever giving way to dark secrets. Lesur has also a primitive quality, as evidenced in his *Suite Médiévale* for flute, harps, violin, viola and cello where he borrows authentic old themes and, while trying to preserve their character, speaks his own language, combining and reconditioning them without deceit. This feature marks the characteristic of most of the fifty scores Lesur has written to this day. They reveal a sincere musician, fond of clarity, hostile to facile exterior effects, to the excesses of the advance guard as well as to stilted formulae.

Lesur has also written for the organ where he proves himself the spiritual disciple of Tournemire: *La Vie intérieure, Scène de la Passion, In Paradisum* are works in which he uses liturgical designs which bestow modal flavor upon his music and allow him to utilize bitonality.

Of the four composers of *La Jeune France*, Lesur is the only one whose musical work is devoid of literary or philosophical preoccupation.

———

YVES BAUDRIER, born in Paris, February 11, 1906, in contrast to Lesur is of the four the one most plagued by extramusical ideas, by the problems of lending these ideas expression in music and by ways and means through which music can find added resonance and extension. He is most of all an academician, a philosopher and lawyer. His musical erudition is almost entirely the result of autodidacticism. As mentioned, to a certain degree he can be considered the theorist of the group when it started, and the manifesto of *La Jeune France*, of which he was the chief editor, undoubtedly reflects his personal views: reincarnation of music in man. As such his music does not allow extraneous subject matters or facts to impress themselves on the score. However, while there may be a difference of opinion as to whether it is to be called just descriptive or pictorial, program music, the titles themselves sufficiently reveal his attitude. *Raz de Sein* is a symphonic poem to which the author was inspired by the dramatic aspect of the ocean. Here the two ideas of the tragic desolation of the wastelands of Brittany and the fatality of the sea current clash, and thus serve as a pretext for drawing an analogy between landscape and emotion. *Le Musicien dans la Cité* is another symphonic poem. It expresses an artist's feelings as he experiences a modern city during a walk by night. The same holds true for his First Symphony based solely on the expression of his temperament at a given moment and systematically banishing all purely formal development. All its structure derived from the momentary play of fantasy. Like Messiaen and Lesur, Baudrier does not believe in the necessity of formal limitations *a priori*. And — this is perhaps a natural result of his autodidacticism — he is afraid that the musical problem could be victimized by purely technical aspects. Technique, as he sees it, leads music to sterile formalism. He observes that under the onslaught of romanticism and impressionism the spontaneous creative expression has renewed the vocabulary of music. To him "the problem is first a spiritual order, then psychological, finally technical." Therefore, in his case we need not look for a system of writing or procedure. "I do not believe," he says, "that a fixed manner of writing can be of benefit to the science of music which is in perpetual development of its dialectic means, because, above all, that science is an artistic matter."

Thus we find in Baudrier, too, the main concern of *La Jeune France:* sincerity.

IV

WE MUST NOW EXAMINE
a certain number of composers who do
not subscribe, as those previously discussed, to one or more ideas held in
common by a group or school. This, in
effect, is the majority of those presently
working in France and, in view of
their number, we are forced to be
selective and can deal only with the
most significant individuals. In general,
these composers follow tradition, though
some testify to real independence

and sometimes possess vital audacity.

They are quite difficult to classify and we have found no better way than that of grouping them chronologically. Nevertheless, they can be allocated to two categories: those stemming from the *Conservatoire National de Paris,* and those whose education has been less rigorous *(Schola Cantorum,* provincial conservatories, private instruction, etc.) It is noteworthy to state that the individualists of both groups are isolated not only in attitude and aesthetic outlook, but also in their reaction to influences: altogether these influences seem to make themselves felt much less conspicuously than in the case of composers who belong to the established groups.

Let us first examine some of the composers of the first category whose background is the *Conservatoire National de Paris.*

JACQUES IBERT (born 1890, Paris; *Premier Grand Prix de Rome,* 1919; director of Villa Medici in Rome since 1936) is a pupil of Gédalge and Vidal. He is a classical musician through and through, more than may appear at first glance. A friend of Honegger and Darius Milhaud at the *Conservatoire,* he did not imitate their boldness, but expressed himself in a language flavored with a certain modernism, yet deeply preserving the mark of tradition. Knowledge, elegance and ingenuity are the characteristics of his very large output which extends into all fields of music, from grand opera via string quartet and concerto to the simplest piano miniature.

GEORGES MIGOT (born 1891, Paris) is one of the most remarkable men of his generation. This composer, a humanist at a time humanism is rare, is also a painter, an engraver, a writer, a philosopher, an

83

aesthetician and a teacher: each one of these specialties would suffice wholly to absorb an individual. Nobody is more independent — and with what modesty! — than this man who, seemingly belonging to an earlier epoch, despises the fashion of the day. A pupil of Gédalge, Widor, Guilmant and Vierne, he hews back to the most profound traditions of French genius. In him we find something of the saint, the scholar, the craftsman. Bold without showing off, he has to his credit a considerable number of works, full of daring. They betray a genuineness and circumspection reminding us of the contributions of the medieval craftsmen of buildings, sculptures or stained glass windows. For him there is no systematic vocabulary, even though he stresses Gregorian modality which preferably he utilizes in a technique re-echoing the art of the contrapuntalists; he also makes ascetic use of the *unison*. Among his most significant works are: *Le Livre des Danceries* for piano, violin and flute; the twelve concert etudes *Zodiaque* for piano; the symphonic fresco *Agrestides*; *La Jungle* for organ and orchestra; the psalm *Coeli enarrant*, and the *Poèmes du Breugnon* (Tristan, Klingsor).

In one of his most recent works, *Saint Germain d'Auxerre*, an a cappella oratorio for four soloists and three mixed choirs, he has given us his best. Here he is heir to the polyphonic masters, vividly illustrating his own definition of his muse: "Music is magic which must satisfy the feeling and the ear simultaneously." In this work one finds his faith, his feeling, his intelligence and his capacity for work. His understanding of French temperament as it persists throughout the centuries is given full expression. The same holds true in the brief oratorio *l'Annonciation* where the subject, so often treated by painters, is set to music for the first time. As Jean Huré has written so correctly, "this is neither an extremist nor a reactionary but a classic who looks upon the past not as a rich arsenal from which to draw ready-made pieces at small expense, but, on the contrary, as a creator desirous of adding a new link to the already long chain of music."

Scarcely the same can be said about JEAN RIVIER (born 1896, Villemonble). This pupil of Jean Gallon and Caussade demonstrates his spontaneity in a robust counterpoint and a vigorous rhythmic language. Fond of classicism, form, proportion, balance, economy of means, sobriety in development and clarity, he thereby accents even more the rough and rugged sides of his language. "The will toward form," he says, "means abhorrence of complication and pathos." His desire for earnestness — even though his musical comedy *Vénitienne,* his *Ouverture pour un Don Quichotte* with its jazz effects, and his Violin Concerto, full of gaiety and humor, may reveal an artist who knows how to smile — is evident in two string quartets and, above all, in five symphonies (the second, third and fourth for string orchestra belong to the most interesting pages of contemporary music). There is also the lofty and austere *Psaume LVI,* an excerpt from the Psalms of David. These works contain his real message. With respect to technique, he states: "I have no harmonic system, no preconceived idea concerning the use of this or that harmony. I employ for each work unconsciously the vocabulary it demands."

A lover of monumental frescoes and of romanticism is PIERRE CAPDEVILLE (born 1906, Paris), a pupil of Vidal and d'Indy, whose range of admiration runs from Wagner to Stravinsky, passing through Debussy, Strauss, Roussel and Schmitt. He, too, is an independent who refuses to recognize any system but who borrows from all those elements which lend themselves to whatever he wishes to express. Expression to him is "the essence of art whose mission it is to interpret the divine as well as the human, and which should lead us all at once to both sides of things and beings." To him art is a ritual. He never considers it just an aesthete's pastime. His style, whether harmonic or contrapuntal, is the bearer of what he wishes to express and, like form, determines the work: here, too, there are no preconceived theories. This is the kind of sincerity we encounter in his songs on lyrics by Rimbaud, Apollinaire, Péguy and Baudelaire, and in his sonatas for viola and piano, violin and cello, flute and viola, and, most of all, in his large symphonic frescoes, particularly in *La Tragédie de Peregrinos*. The latter is a cantata with narration based on a text by Charles Exbrayat. *L'Ile Rouge* is written to a poem by Serge Moreux, a vast choral composition on the order of a "documentary and adventure film" about the geography, and the ethnic and political history of Madagascar. *Invocation* for the death of a young Spartan is a noble score with romantic fervor. It was written to glorify a friend's act of heroism in the mountains and to honor his memory. Unity of style, power and sobriety are the prominent qualities of this music.

YVONNE DESPORTES (born 1907, Cobourg; *Prix de Rome,* 1932) is a Paul Dukas pupil. She seems to prefer music based on concrete subjects to absolute

(Piano Quintet, Variations for violin and piano, *Variations Symphoniques* for piano and orchestra). This preference is revealed in works of a certain kinship with Ravel, such as the symphonic poems *Hercule et les Géants, Résurrection* and *Le Rondeau du Voyageur,* and scores devoted to the theatre such as *Le Rossignol et l'Orvet, Les Sept Péchés Capitaux* and *Maître Cornelius.*

"Music seems to me above all an art of feeling in which theories, technique, and purely intellectual exercises are cumbersome accessories," says HENRI-ETTE ROGET (born 1910, Bastia, Corsica; *Second Grand Prix de Rome,* 1933). As a pianist and organist, she has devoted most of her composition to the two keyboard instruments. She has a feeling for breadth of idea and for development, and she possesses a strength for form. Here is neither feminine fastidiousness nor pretended virility, but the flavor of a fresh poetry evoked by concise means. This is suggested by her *Concerto da Camera* for piano and orchestra, her *Sinfonia Anderrana* for piano and orchestra and her *Concerto Sicilien* in four parts. The latter does not take refuge in folksong material nor does it pretend to recreate the atmosphere of Sicily. Instead, it seeks to conjure up the events of the Sicilian campaign of 1943. As an organist she belongs to what has become known as the "colorists," justifying this classification with a *Fantaisie sur des Thèmes Hébraïques* and, even more, with *Montanyas del Rosello,* two beautiful scores of Mediterranean flavor for organ and orchestra.

MARC VAUBOURGOIN (born 1907, Caudéran; *Premier Grand Prix de Rome,* 1930) is of all the Dukas pupils the one who has profited most by his master's teachings. Without being reactionary, his First Symphony, his Concerto for orchestra with cello obbligato and his Quintet for wind instruments rank him as follower of the purest French classicism. The vigorous symphonist, who is also known as a conductor, reveres Stravinsky's genius, yet is equally attracted by the neglected works of old masters: thus we are indebted to him for unabbreviated performances of Scarlatti and Destouches operas.

TONY AUBIN (born 1907, Paris; *Premier Grand Prix de Rome,* 1930) is Vaubourgoin's twin, so to speak, and one of the more prominent Dukas disciples. In his work we discover the influence, well assimilated, of Franck, Dukas, Fauré and Ravel. From Franck and Dukas he has inherited the love for well balanced large forms, from Fauré and Ravel subtle harmonies and a supreme elegance. While he has composed a "scherzo fantastique" *La Chasse Infernale,* inspired by the story of the Chevalier Pécopin in Victor Hugo's *Contes du Rhin,* and has penned a *Suite Danoise* and *Cressida,* he is drawn by temperament to absolute music, as is testified by his remarkable *Symphonie Romantique.* The composer himself says that the latter has no literary background, that "its romanticism consists solely of the search for a lyrical expression to serve simple form." The symphony is in three movements built on themes of great nobility. It is of grandiose atmosphere, of pure lyricism, of vast and vigorous construction, and it shuns facile and conventional effects of oratory.

JEAN LANGLAIS (born 1907, La Fontenelle) is a pupil of André Marchal, Marcel Dupré and Paul Dukas, and an organist of St. Clothilde. He has proved himself a very fertile composer. He often seeks inspiration in folk music or in Gregorian patterns, which give a modal flavor to his music. His early organ works have a distinctive poetic climate: *Trois Poèmes Evangéliques, Trois Paraphrases Grégoriennes*. Later his art became more gentle, more relaxed, spontaneous and on a higher intellectual plane. Examples are *Vingt quatre Pièces, Deux Offertoires pour tous les Temps* and, above all, his First Symphony, which is remarkable for the vigor of style and structure.

Another organist, GASTON LITAIZE (born 1909, Ménil-sur-Belvitte; *Grand Prix de Rome*), a pupil of Vierne, a teacher at the Institute for Blind Children and chief organist at St. François Xavier, has an understanding for expansive musical construction. His orientation, however, is not so much toward the exploitation of classical forms as it is toward the enrichment of his language.

This results in a novel treatment of the theme in ancient modes, as for instance in his *Grand' Messe* and his *Messe basse.*

———

First to be discussed of the group of composers not trained at the *Conservatoire National* is ROLAND MANUEL (born 1891, Paris). He participated, off and on, in the new movements after World War I and therefore has been called "the seventh of the *Six.*" His natural tendencies, his education and his culture did not allow him decisively to join the ranks of those then considered revolutionists. After studies with Droeghmans and at the *Schola* with Roussel and Sériey, he took up composition with Ravel and has remained not only the latter's most authoritative interpreter but, to a degree, his spiritual heir with respect to classical French tradition. "If music had seemed a problem to me," he once wrote, "I think I never would have composed." This explains his opposition to everything systematic and that his aesthetic creed is independent of any preconceived thought. By his own definition it is only the result of feeling. His is an encyclopedic mind. He is a humanist and an artist hostile to all exaggerations, particularly as to emotion and expression. He stays aloof from anything that could possibly reflect the romantic attitude or reaction to which many of his contemporaries sometimes succumb. His manner of expression betrays descent from the early French clavecinists as well as from Debussy and Ravel. The language is that of his time, however, and he never fails to use the latest technical material. Witness particularly his enchanting comic opera *Isabelle et Pantalon* on a libretto by Max Jacob; a concerto for piano and orchestra; *Elvire,* a ballet on themes by Scarlatti; *Le Diable Amoureux,* a comic opera, and the ballet *l'Ecran des Jeunes Filles* with a smattering of jazz. All these works, including his numerous film scores, are written in a clear and sober manner which sometimes employs biting harmonies, great instrumental ingenuity and always reflects solicitude for the form.

LOUIS BEYDTS (born 1895, Bordeaux) continues the tradition of French operetta, following André Messager and Reynaldo Hahn. His only teacher Vaubourgoin has made of him a classical and strict harmonist; his admiration for Gounod, Fauré and Massenet as well as his great melodic gifts explain his personality. Beydts' output is almost exclusively devoted to the voice, operettas and songs, and he is thoroughly familiar with the resources of vocalism. He also has a very keen sensitivity for the melodic inflection of the French language and its subtle accents, permitting him a flawless prosody whether he sets to music librettos by Duvernois or Sascha Guitry *(Moineau, Les Canards Mandarins, La S.A.D.M.P.)* or the poems by Marcelline Desbordes Valmore, Joachim du Bellay and Guillaume Apolinaire on which he bases his songs.

MARCEL DELANNOY (born 1898, La Ferté Alais) knows how to link the old and the new, the popular and the scholarly. While he has taken the advice of Jean Gallon, Gédalge and Honegger and is not altogether an autodidact, he owes his artistic growth mainly to independent orientation. It is difficult to find in his music the predominant influence of any particular master. It is a highly personalized music. The only discernible, obvious and profound influence is that of the folksong whose melodic and rhythmic elements appear throughout his writing, just as do certain features borrowed from jazz and South American music, particularly the rhumba. Immediately famous upon the performance of his comic opera *Le Poirier de Misère,* which created an uproar but was also a success, he wrote *Le Feu de la Dame,* an interesting attempt at a revival of the old genre of ballet-cantata; then he wrote the ballet *La Pantoufle de Vair;* the comic opera *Ginevra; Puck,* after Shakespeare's *Midsummer Night's Dream,* in an adaptation by André Boll, and finally *Abraham,* an even more complex attempt to wed music, the dance and the theatre than had been *Feu de la Dame.*

In the field of instrumental music, mention must be made of a very solidly constructed symphony, a concerto for piano and orchestra entitled *Concert de Mai,* and particularly of a string quartet in which we recognize his gift for rhythmic and melodic invention, as we find the folklore so characteristic of his inspiration. Here an elegant language, never conventional yet never aggressive, holds sway.

EMMANUEL BONDEVILLE (born 1898, Rouen) also has had very little academic instruction. He has risked the hazards and exhausted the potentials of an artist's life notwithstanding the fact that circumstances prevented him from the complete devotion to music which he would have liked. His art is unencumbered by extreme subtleties and well reflects the temperament of an artist who is naive, robust and simple in a rustic sense. His manner of writing turns out to be most satisfactory, however, when applied to the theatre or to symphonic works as testified by the comic opera *L'Ecole des Maris,* and by *Le Bal des Pendus,* and *Illustrations pour Faust.* A recent comic opera after Gustave Flaubert's *Madame Bovary,* where his style is particularly refined and not without some relationship to Fauré, indicates that he has not yet spoken his last word.

Of the four composers born in the year 1900 and including Henri Barraud, Robert Bernard, Maurice Jaubert and Pierre Octave Ferroud, two must gather our attention.

Like all young musicians from Bordeaux, HENRI BARRAUD studied for a time with Vaubourgoin, but later worked with Louis Aubert. He became one of the founders of *Triton,* a chamber music society which was active in the defense and performance of contemporary music between the wars. Since 1945 he has been chief of the music division of the French radio network *(Radiodiffusion Française)* where much of his effort is devoted to contemporary music. His art is not impeded by literature, rather it is spontaneous and taut, but behind a facade of bashfulness and reserve there hides a real sensitivity. This is proved by the fact that he composes with feeling and without a theory, a matter explained thusly in his own words: "I really feel the work in complete existence even before I have thought of penning it. Patient and prudent quest which leads me to give it, yes, to find for it, its proper form, is the only method I can follow .... Once found, it is difficult to retrace my way to it by remembering the path that led me to invention, and the completed work transforms itself into a mystery the clue to which has been irreparably lost."

From a strictly musical point of view, Barraud renounces no single way of writing and uses any which seem to him suitable for a given occasion. He points out that the main characteristics of his language are frequent use of modal scales, occasional borrowings from folklore, the use of certain common intervals like the tritone, little taste for melodic themes based on chord succession which to him make sense only by imputed roots, a thematic invention with a view to the melodic potentialities rather than to the potential of counterpoint, and, finally, fidelity to tonality.

These are the characteristics of such works as the Symphony, the *Poème pour Orchestre,* the *Impromptus* for piano, the Piano Concerto and the String Quartet. They are typical of the composer's spontaneity and inwardness.

His more recent works, humanized and apparently more expressive, differ to a considerable extent. In an interview covering this later period, Barraud stated: "I esteem the violent passion animating Schmitt's works and the marvelous musical substance which is the mark of Ravel. Nevertheless, I am presently inclined toward less opulent harmonies and fewer juxtaposed chords .... I express only one wish: that my music shall not be classified as either playful or cerebral .... I prefer inward and lyric music which tries to strike a balance between emotions and intellectual pleasures." This he has obviously attained in his great oratorio *Le Mystère des Saints Innocents* on a text of Péguy, and in the brief, moving symphonic poem *Offrande pour une Ombre* written in memory of Maurice Jaubert.

His recent opera *Numance,* first heard at the *Théâtre National de l'Opéra* in Paris in 1955 is undoubtedly his most important work. It is composed to a libretto or rather a dramatic poem by Salvador de Madariaga, a writer who was inspired by the drama which Cervantes had fashioned from the famous episode of Roman history. Barraud has sought — and found — a lyric style, breaking completely with hallowed traditions and conventions of opera. *Numance* is a realistic and human work of great nobility. The composer has not attempted bravura effects, he has not robbed the text of the dramatic values with which his collaborator endowed it. He has limited himself to providing it with a range of expression which is in perfect conformity with each phase of the dramatic action.

PIERRE OCTAVE FERROUD'S career was a very brief one (born 1900, Chasselay, Rhône, he died in 1936 in a car accident in Hungary); notwithstanding he has played a large part in the music of his time, by action as well as output. Due to his initiative, *Triton,* the society for contemporary music, was founded in the thirties with the help of some French and foreign composers of his generation. It acquainted the public with the works of the young school. Even though Ferroud was educated in a somewhat scattered and haphazard manner which could have resulted in amateurishness, he quickly established himself as one of the most earnest composers of his time. He evidences considerable gifts in coining a highly personalized and — for the period — quite novel style, one consisting of factors which he had introduced to the French school of composition. Their home was Central Europe, and his aesthetic beliefs, Middle European, were identical with those of *Triton* which later produced the reactions of *La Jeune France.*

Ferroud, who studied harmony with

Commette, the organist of Lyons, counterpoint with Erb of Strasbourg, and with
Ropartz and Witkowsky, found in Florent
Schmitt not only the master and teacher,
but the ruler of a musical conscience
which best suited his gifts, proclivities
and aspirations. His work reflects an
astonishingly contradictory nature: cold
objectivity and lyric passion, sarcasm and
tenderness, unpolished expression and
gentle conception, keen intellectualism
and dreamy fantasy. These contrasts
undoubtedly would have become less
pronounced had Ferroud's fate allowed
him to mature. However, this uncertainty, this dualism of youth does not
reduce the value of his message. He
remains the custodian of the music of the
robust Florent Schmitt, worthy of the
man from whom he took advice. With
respect to his musical language it is
possible to find the same schism: generous

counterpoint and feeling for subtle harmony. He wrote: "Through counterpoint music attains the universality of which it is the language, whereas harmony always preserves a national color." He has sought contrapuntal ingenuity, scholarly to the point of esoteric scholasticism; yet the most sumptuous harmonies, an amusing, crafty or pleasant modulation would often flow from his pen. This contrast between his defense of contrapuntal sobriety and his instinct for voluptuous harmony is found again in his orchestration. He moves from a piano piece to the rich orchestration of the same work re-echoing sounds favored by Florent Schmitt. This is the case with his suite *Au Parc Monceau,* the orchestral version of which reveals an unusually vigorous symphonic composer; with *Foules* which evokes — without pictorial description — "the rumble of a modern city, the gasping for breath, the beating of the hearts" and, finally, with his Symphony in A, one of the most remarkable edifices of music which the period between the wars has witnessed.

On the other hand, he realized his theoretical principles of objective art in full in his chamber music, and he did so without becoming cerebral: a Sonata for piano and cello in three-part counterpoint with a transparent texture, but at the same time rugged in contour; a Trio for oboe, clarinet and bassoon which seems a bit aggressive considering the year (1933), but the sonority of which has softened with the passage of time; a String Quartet with almost brutal outbursts whose strength reminds us of Hindemith; *Trois Poèmes Intimes de Goethe,* set on German words and entitled "vocal sonatina" by the composer. The tone of the latter is more expressive and human. Neither should we forget his comic opera *Chirurgie,* after Chekhov, where his sarcastic pen and his comically cruel whims are given free rein.

V

*T*O COMPLETE THE PICTURE
let us glance at the young composers
now between twenty and forty years
old and discuss some of those born after
1910, who either are promising or already
have given proof of their abilities. When
they came upon the scene they found a
musical world of indecision, confusion
and division. They had at their disposal
the most diversified and perfected
weapons with which to continue the
battle: tonality, polytonality, modality,

atonality, twelve-tone technique and the combinations of all of these.

As before, we again have composers independent of any schools and, on the other hand, groups within which the composers practicing the twelve-tone or related techniques are particularly prominent.

————

JEHAN ALAIN (born 1911, St. Germain en Laye, died 1940 on the field of battle). Norbert Dufourcq has called him "the Grigny of our time . . . like him an organist's son, a precocious composer, and gone before entering his fourth decade." At the *Conservatoire* he was a pupil of Dukas, Roger Ducasse and Marcel Dupré, subsequent to instruction from his father, an organist of St. Germain. Here we have one more example of a true independent: a virtuoso of individualism, freedom of thought and technique. No school, no system can lay claim to him. In his case there is nothing of the uncertainty of youth: he has always drawn his manner of expression from most diverse sources. This he was able to do thanks to miraculous gifts, a prodigious cultural background, an indefatigable inquisitiveness, a quick mind, readiness for work and a boundless imagination. His was a natural and unaffected imagination, without studied attitude, governed only by a feeling for every moment, every idea, every being and every thing. He was an unusual man and artist. He was also, and above all, a Christian whose work is that of a great and sturdy believer who has no need of literature to sing of his faith.

Indeed he never needs conventional means to express himself, whether in spiritual or technical realms. As to the latter point his liberty is extreme in that measure bars, tonality, modality, etc. to him are but simple tools. As to form, he would use the most classical, such as prelude, fugue and chorale, with more or less strictness but, on the whole, with freedom. He seems to illustrate and realize Liszt's wish: "The ideal would be that each subject matter had its own form from which it cannot be separated."

The influences of Franck, Tournemire, Dupré and Messiaen here detectable, though they are real, are without great importance; the speaker remains Jehan Alain. He has a bit of Schumann's nature, and one is reminded of the German word *phantasieren,* synonyms for which, according to the dictionary, are to dream, to indulge in fancies, to be in ecstasy, to ramble and to improvise. According to those who knew him well, his organ improvisations were stupendous. He would never seek refuge in the convenient formulae and commonplaces so thoroughly exploited by many excellent organists.

This shows itself in his *Postlude pour l'Office des Complies,* his hymn *Te lucis ante terminum* and particularly in his *Litanies,* which are not only the summit of his art, but of all contemporary organ literature. Let us also mention *Trois Danses,* his musical last will, a triptych where he juxtaposes joy and disappointment and the crowning glory of hope.

Another remarkable organist of this generation is JEAN-JACQUES GRUE-NENWALD (born 1911, Anneey; pupil of Marcel Dupré and Buesser, *Premier Second Grand Prix de Rome,* 1939). His art is austere and romantic at the same time. The tone sometimes borders on violence, as in his *Hymnes aux Mémoires*

Héroïques and *Hymnes à la Splendeur des Etoiles* where he employs polytonality and polymodality. His Biblical symphonic poem *Bethsabée* in four parts contains some very strange rhythmic effects; he develops a vigorous feeling for lyricism and pathos, reaching greatness and force in the final hymn.

JEAN FRANCAIX (born 1912, Le Mans), a piano student at the *Conservatoire,* studied harmony and composition with Nadia Boulanger and is one of the most prodigiously gifted composers of the new group. While his inventiveness does not undergo much change, his workmanship testifies to surprising facility, so that he can handle, with ease and gracefulness, opera *(La Main de Gloire),* oratorio *(Apocalypse de Saint Jean),* ballet *(Beach, Scuola di ballo, Le Roi Nu,* etc.), as well as concerto, chamber music and piano pieces. It has been said that he is like a son of Jacques Ibert. His language is, in the last analysis, that of a classical composer who, however, is not afraid of using the spice of modern harmony with which he flavors works all logically developed, concise, pleasant, easy-going, with no other aim than to arouse pleasure. Their common motto might very well be Henri de Régnier's delightful epigram inscribed by Ravel on the score of his *Valses Nobles et Sentimentales:* "The delicious, ever novel pleasure of useless occupation."

HENRI DUTILLEUX (born 1916, Angers), a pupil of Jean and Noël Gallon and of Buesser, obtained a *Prix de Rome* in 1938. He is another true independent who escapes all system, all schools and watchwords. He is a classicist with a predilection for musical architecture and counterpoint, but his harmonic language makes him an artist of his time.

If he must be linked with the past — from which he stems, since he is no revolutionary — one may say that as a harmonist he is a descendant of Fauré and Ravel without actually succumbing to the influence of either. Only his harmonic attitude, or rather his attitude toward harmony, is comparable to Fauré or Ravel, his basic vocabulary is highly personalized and reveals a kind of unrealized atonal feeling. In form he is closer to the d'Indy type of conception, no matter how he differs from that master otherwise, and particularly as regards his asceticism.

His most significant works are a *Suite de Danses,* a *Danse Fantastique* drawn from a *Symphonie de Danses* and, particularly, a piano sonata which deserves special mention. The latter is one of the very few in that form to originate in the most recent epoch. It proves itself worthy of its great tradition. It is furthermore the most accomplished work this young composer has created. It is of classical dimensions: an initial *allegro con moto* with two themes; a slow movement of song form refraining from exaggerated effusion; a final movement consisting of a hymn with four variations whose sonorous effects are adroitly handled to bring the work to an intensely luminous climax.

His Symphony of 1951 confirms the originality of his vocabulary, his ability in scoring and his sensitivity to musical texture. It also confirms that here is one who avoids speaking when he has nothing to say.

The *Progressivists* is a school which has produced more noise than works. It first appeared in France in 1948 under the name of *Association Française des Musiciens Progressistes* when a group of young composers — including a few older men — banded together in order to submit to the Soviet principles of art as such were defined in the Andrei Idanov manifesto.

In reality it does not appear that this doctrine has so far greatly inspired even the militant composers who seemed so fully convinced of the necessity for condemning "an art which isolates itself from life by burying itself in the mysteries of formalism and pessimism." It also postulates that music can have value only if it expresses the life of the people and their fight for a better world and for peace. Such music — it is contended — must be written for the masses.

The school has brought forth only a

few rather mediocre works by Louis Durey, a veteran formerly of the *Six*, and by such young composers as Serge Nigg, a fugitive from twelve-tone music, and Michel Philippot.

———

The musical group *Le Zodiaque* was born in 1947 as a reaction against systems, prejudices, habits and fashions. It became the rallying point of some young composers who wished to affirm their complete independence, and who rejected regimentation of any kind. They protested against the neo-romanticism of *La Jeune France,* against the strict discipline of twelve-tone technique and against the principles of the *Progressivists.* This attitude, a somewhat negative program of action, constituted their point of departure. They gradually

121

became aware of the positive side of their movement which they define as follows: restore to Western music of Mediterranean vintage its normal manner, which is neither the romanticism nor the intellectuality of Mid-European music; react against these two influences which sometimes have invaded our music and deflected it from its purely Occidental and Latin traditions; restore the genealogical tree of these traditions and, with their help, renew the sources as much as possible. Therefore the members of the *Zodiaque* are not confined to classicism nor do they propose neo-classicism, but rather an art which is nurtured by medieval traditions as far as the spiritual outlook is concerned, but, of course, not with respect to vocabulary and construction.

In practice this art results in works for small instrumental ensembles — a sign of the materially difficult times for young composers today. The simplicity of the musical material used gives to their music a certain roughness, a crudeness and a violence which reminds us of similar elements in Rouault's painting. They do not altogether exclude lyricism. On the contrary, when lyricism appears, it is not toned down.

The common aesthetic feeling of the group, which, on the whole, is expressed by a demand for liberty, involves absolute freedom of language. All problems of vocabulary and method are ignored, or, at best, use is made of elements derived from a method. There is a pronounced tendency toward universality and humanism, indicated in the symbolic name of *Zodiaque*. The group tries to bring about a synthesis of the different elements of style at their disposal, such as tonality, atonality, modality, polymodality, twelve-tone technique, etc. Problems of form are not recognized either, although the concern for audible symmetry often leads some of these composers close to classical structures.

The membership of *Zodiaque* is eloquent proof of its independent and anticonformist spirit in that five are Parisians whereas three are foreigners.

MAURICE OHANA, a British subject of Spanish descent (born 1914, Gibraltar) is a Parisian by education and choice. At the *Schola Cantorum* he was a pupil of Lesur. A sublimated Spanish influence is found in his music. The best example is his splendid *Plainte pour Ignacio Sanchoz Mejiaz* for narrator, baritone, chorus and chamber orchestra, after a beautiful poem by Garcia Lorca. Here we can discern no search for pictorial folklorism, no use of folklore elements, yet the spirit of folk music permeates a work whose musical

material, themes, harmonies and rhythms
is essentially original. He has written also
a Concerto for guitar (or harpsichord) and
orchestra, a Sonatina for voice and
orchestra, the ballet *L'Auberge Enchantée*
taken from an episode in *Don Quixote,*
and a *Suite pour un Mimodrame* for
chamber orchestra. We also have a
number of excellent scores for the theatre
from his pen.

STANISLAS SKROVATCHEVSKI
(born 1920), a Polish composer, became a
member of the group during his long stay
in France (he has now returned to the
country of his birth). His education and
inclinations make him come closest,
among the group, to classical ideas. His
main contributions include a score for
voice and twenty-three instruments,
excerpts of the *Cantique des Cantiques.*
It is a very impressive document of
Zodiaque aesthetics. He also wrote a

Symphony for string orchestra and a *Prélude et Fugue* which reveals his stylistic vigor.

SERGIO DE CASTRO (born 1921), an Argentine of Spanish descent, was a pupil of Manuel de Falla whose later, highly simplified style influenced de Castro's beginnings. His main works are *Homage à Manuel de Falla* for orchestra, and a Trio for piano, violin and flute.

PIERRE DE LA FOREST DIVONNE (born 1926, Paris) started as a pupil of Olivier Messiaen, of whom frequent traces may be found in both music and spiritual outlook, and then was taught by Daniel Lesur. His inspiration is frequently mystical: *Gethsemani,* an oratorio for chorus, narration and orchestra; *De Profundis,* a large chant in which strings dominate the orchestra, and *Messe pour le Temps de la Passion* for chorus and organ. He is the composer also of a string symphony and of a concertino for piano and strings.

ALAIN BERMAT (born 1926), a pupil of Daniel Lesur, seems to be a profound artist who, however, is not as yet in full control of the expressive means he wishes to employ. He has written a *Prélude* for symphonic orchestra, interesting for its development and the breadth of its expression; *Choral* for orchestra, betraying a vigorous lyricism; a String Quartet, and various songs to poems by P. J. Toulet.

————

From the preceding discussion to this one means going from one extreme to the other. But let us look a little further back.

After World War I the Austrian composer Arnold Schoenberg laid the foundations for a new method of musical composition — the tone-row method applied within the framework of twelve-tone atonalism. He immediately attracted the attention of the young French composers. Darius Milhaud and Francis Poulenc even went to Vienna to see the man who had reversed the time-honored tonal principle and had dissolved its concept with all its implications. They wanted to meet Schoenberg's first disciples, who equally had aroused the curiosity and admiration of Western musicians: Alban Berg, Anton von Webern and Egon Wellesz. These moves at that time were born from simple curiosity and remained without consequence. None of these French composers was really tempted to impose upon himself the discipline of Schoenberg and, in the ensuing years, after the first shock effect, the new method was no longer discussed in France, at least not as a method for Frenchmen. Yet, in reality, French composers continued to admire and to welcome the works of the Viennese school.

Suddenly, in the forties, the "twelve-tone fire" was rekindled by a number of young composers who took their first steps into the musical world. They were mainly products of Olivier Messiaen's class at the *Conservatoire*. It should not be inferred that Messiaen himself had guided them to such technique. It is quite likely, however, that he himself and the high level of his teaching had wakened his students to a considerable concern for the mastery for which they felt a calling. In this concern for a solution to the contemporary problem of musical development they were, of course, in constant search for a new means of expression to advance the musical vocabulary. It seems that Messiaen's students did not find the new means in the system applied by their master. Therefore the majority believed that possibly it could be found in the twelve-tone technique to which they began to subscribe more or less whole-heartedly.

Strangely enough, the rigid dogmatism of the method did not seem to embarrass the young French twelve-tone composers, notwithstanding the fact that the French opponents had shown an antagonistic attitude including a no less systematic rejection. Indeed, it is noteworthy that the adherents were in favor of the most rigid employment of the method, thus becoming direct followers of von Webern. With some, this unreserved rigidity leaves room for the type of lyrical expressionism reminiscent of Berg.

The historic circumstances under which the French twelve-tone school came into being and developed seem quite rigorously to have conditioned that formation and development. We are in the forties. Seven young people study harmony in Messiaen's class, counterpoint and fugue in Caussade's: Pierre Boulez, Serge Nigg, Maurice Le Roux, Yvonne Loriod, Yvette Grimaux, J. L. Martinet and Bernard Flavigny. They are all about seventeen or eighteen years old, all except Martinet, who is about ten years older and has already studied with Ducasse. All that happened before 1939 means nothing to them; their age and the war with its spiritual and material consequences have isolated them completely from the immediate past. They enter Messiaen's class in a state of almost perfect musical virginity. Messiaen is to give them the most extraordinary type of instruction, so liberal, so daring, so new that it is as unacademic as it is untraditional. They study the classical masters, tc be sure, but become equally familiar with the Indian or Balinese music to which they listen on records at the *Musée de l'Homme*. They make the acquaintance of ancient modes, of Schoenberg, Bartok and Stravinsky, composers whose works Messiaen analyzes for them with greatest authority.

These young people can never forget the dazzling analysis of *Sacre du Printemps* which lasted almost eight hours! In brief, they obtain unusual instruction with everything geared to develop their inquisitiveness.

This thorough inquisitiveness develops as much as does their concern for the discovery of a new language which would be a reaction against the surface art of the composers "between the wars." It is natural for them to unite under the banner of the twelve-tone technique, the more so since Yvette Grimaux, one of these students, was by nature attracted to the dodekaphonic system and had a considerable influence on the group. The twelve-tone system provides them with the means of radically changing the vocabulary. It also furnishes the rules with which they feel they must surround themselves. This need for authority and discipline is undoubtedly in line with the climate of those years: a sign of the confusion then quite common with a large part of French youth. In 1945 most of these young people deserted Messiaen's class to attach themselves to the St. John the Baptist of Schoenberg's "religion," namely René Leibowitz (born in Warsaw in 1913). He was a pupil of von Webern, had lived in France since 1925, and had become known as a composer, critic, teacher, musicologist, and the author of *Schoenberg and His School.*

Of these seven students, only four have

attempted professional careers as composers: Boulez, Nigg, Le Roux and Martinet. Yvonne Loriod, who has composed but little, has remained faithful to Messiaen's principles and has become his most authoritative pianistic interpreter. Yvette Grimaux, also a pianist, and endowed with an exceptional musical mind, has made a career as soloist by devoting herself chiefly to the performance of modern music, as has Bernard Flavigny.

PIERRE BOULEZ (born 1925, Montbrison) undoubtedly is the most gifted of this group, and his personality seems to dominate it to this day. Of rustic stock, he had intended to devote himself to science, took courses in mathematics and prepared himself for the Polytechnic Institute before finding his way to music. From the beginning he was quite attracted by the music of the Far East,

Java, Indochina, and by its complex rhythms. He has been a pupil first of Messiaen and then of Leibowitz, and has enjoyed the sponsorship of Honegger. Heugel published his music. He now seems to orient himself toward neo-surrealism and might be considered a musical counterpart to the poet René Char.

Boulez is a prodigious performer on the *Ondes Martenot* and on the piano, where he displays a rare virtuosity based on the highly original keyboard technique required in his own scores. Virtuosity is encountered in his writing, too. The latter reveals an altogether exceptional ear. Due to the strictness of the twelve-tone technique employed, it is a direct offspring of von Webern with whom the composer shares antiromantic leanings. This relationship is interesting to note because von Webern, even though he

135

developed the system to its last consequence, was far from shutting the door
behind him. Boulez appears to go beyond
von Webern and to breathe new life into
twelve-tone music by literally applying
it to excess. At any rate, he employs it
with such virtuosity and subtlety, with
such inventiveness and range that the
result is nothing short of astounding.
According to Maurice Le Roux, one of his
colleagues and friends in twelve-tone
technique:

> "He is not only possessed with a
> concern for ever-new sonorities, as
> preached by the Schoenberg school,
> but also by that for form and even
> more by the balance between
> rhythmic and melodic opulence. In a
> way he has unmasked the rhythmic
> paucity of the twelve-tone vocabu-
> lary and, by drawing the conclusions
> from Messiaen's teachings, has dis-

covered the secret rhythmic laws of atonality."

Boulez has composed chamber music works (in particular a Quartet for *Ondes Martenot*), vocal music and, above all, piano music. His recent Second Piano Sonata constitutes his most advanced attainment and is an "accurate interpretation of our period, extremely subtle, brutal, bold, hypersensitive, feverish, but organized, coherent, rigid and precise."

His main works, besides the two piano sonatas, are a cantata, *Le Soleil des Eaux*, on poems by René Char; *Polyphonie X*, for seventeen instruments; *Le Marteau sans Maître* and *Livre de Quatuor*. The sonatas and the cantata are works of experimentation. In *Polyphonie X* this experimentation goes quite far in that Boulez here carries the series to its extreme consequence: the order in which the different instruments begin is subjugated to the strict discipline of dode-kaphonic technique.

Le Marteau and the *Livre* are mature works no longer of an experimental nature. Here Boulez' personality asserts itself. *Le Marteau sans Maître,* a kind of cantata for female voice and seven instruments on poems by René Char, and *Livre de Quatuor* for string quartet are scores which distinguish themselves by the utmost variety of sonorous effects, by great sobriety in opulence, by transparency in sumptuousness — all qualities which are irresistibly reminiscent of the lasting classicism of French art. Here we find the economy of means, balance and luminous plenitude so typically French. Boulez terminates and at the same time denies what in Debussy had been called impressionism, but which is not a Debussyan phenomenon alone; rather it is one of the constant attributes of French musical perceptiveness throughout the centuries. The striking feature of these two works is the constant flow of unusual and refined inventiveness. A novel, subtle and profound lyricism is inherent in the structural outlines of the music comparable to the lyricism of classical monuments that is inseparable from their lines and their heights. This lyricism is particularly accented in the *Livre de Quatuor,* a work in which the affinity with Debussy is discernible — a score far from being watered-down impressionism. This is a situation similar to Debussy's own invocation of the classics without descending thereby to a banal neo-classicism. In fact, Boulez achieves a synthesis of Debussy's and von Webern's discoveries by making more extended use of their innovations and treating them in an original and novel manner.

MAURICE LE ROUX (born 1923,

Paris) has worked with Messiaen, Ducasse and, temporarily, with Leibowitz. He is a composer, conductor, critic, musicologist and professor of music history. His is an encyclopedic and humanist mind. Eager for novelty, he has thoroughly assimilated Messiaen's teachings, has profoundly absorbed the influence of Bartok and has even tried his hand at *musique concrète*. He remains convinced, however, that the solution today lies in atonality. His style, just as Boulez', is rigid but, contrary to Boulez, he does not want to inhibit his own temperament, one with such potential for romanticism. He has written *Inventions* for two parts and a piano sonata, songs to poems by Henri Michaux, five-part a cappella Psalms after texts by Patrice de la Tour du Pin, two *Mimes* for chamber orchestra, *Le Voyage en Grande Garabagne* for orchestra after Henri Michaux, and a ballet after *Le Petit Prince* by Saint Exupéry.

JEAN LOUIS MARTINET (born 1914, Sainte-Bazeille, Lot-et-Garonne) has approached atonality more artificially than spontaneously, and basically seems fond of tonality. His first works show Debussy's influence, and the later ones preserve quite strongly the mark of Stravinsky, Bartok and, above all, of his teacher Messiaen. Among his current output mention must be made of a sonata, songs with orchestra, and an orchestral work of great breadth, *Orphée,* a large triptych in which he reveals his forceful temperament, obvious feeling for construction and taste for dense sonorities, often excessively employed. In this score Martinet leaves behind some of the influences hitherto displayed. Seemingly he wishes to attain balance, but it cannot truthfully be said that he has attained it.

141

VI

ERMANY AT THE BEGINNING
of the nineteenth century had assumed
the leadership in the musical life of
Europe; at the end of the last century,
during the period of Impressionism, she
had lost her key position to our country,
which meant a decentralization of all
musical art, a decentralization of no mean
proportions. That factor, perhaps more
than any other, attracted the attention of
at least all cultural circles of the
Western World to France, from which

country painters, composers and literary personalities expected the decisive aesthetic impulses before and after the First World War.

In the twilight situation marked by decentralization, on the one hand, and by what we called ossification on the other, we recognized the ever-growing significance of the Russian, i. e. the Stravinskyan influence, and that of the Austrian: Schoenberg, or the twelve-tone music. The *Arceuil School,* as we have seen, was a group of individualists gathering under the banner of the revered Satie. Neither was *La Jeune France* unified by musical aspirations; rather the element which bound them together was an extramusical one: reaction against the *Triton* and the abstractivist leanings of Middle Europeans. It furnished a document, as we see it in retrospect, of that French spirit which especially our friends from abroad identify with our proverbial detestation of regimentation. The positive side, that of strength instead of negation, and sheer independence in the chase for novel expressive means and a new musical vocabulary, is embodied in Messiaen, experimenter, to be sure, but the objective analyst of classical taste and tradition in our French music: we called him not the head of a movement, nor could we see in him a master *per se,* but a passionate seeker and searcher.

The lack of a system is both the characteristic feature and the weakness of the young composers, as, in a different sense — the reader will remember — it was of "the Independents" in whose works less of an awareness of the tradition is found than on the part of the "established" groups.

World War II not only hampered, paralyzed and even killed a musical life which had been exciting, controversial and ever so multifaceted, it also made an end of international exchange and cultural rapprochement. Only in the last years have the countries of the West come closer together, and many threads now run from France to the other music-minded elements and circles of Western Europe, the United States, and in fact to and from the Eastern world. This experience of internationalism — the moving together of cultural units of most diverse ambitions — is not only most gratifying, it is at the same time the most remarkable advent in the music of our country as it is in that of others. Whether under this influence we will revaluate our own traditions and tastes, reconquer romantic realms, broaden our already considerable antiromantic or perhaps even cerebral leanings, or become subdued in a Dionysian ecstasy over one-worldism or, the opposite, in a perhaps impractical attempt at counteracting, through art and music, our epoch of ever-growing materialism and our development of technical weapons and atomic reactors, who knows? We have survived the catastrophes of World War II and that of the catastrophe which followed.

Almost all other questions remain unanswered at this time. We in France have plentiful production and creativity. Yet it is safe to say no one could possibly appraise with objectivity the value of the new. Therefore we must be careful with all appraisal of contemporary, and especially of the most recent, tendencies and confine ourselves to recording, to observation and, as we judge, to statements made with tentativeness and reservation. Where we are wrong, *tempus,* never resting, never stationary, will correct us, and the future will consider this record, this brief commentary, as but one testimony born from one who believes himself to be a watchful observer in 1957.

———